Show me your garden
and I shall tell you what you are.

ALFRED AUSTIN

For the year

____

Country Living

Country Garden Journal

Additional credits and acknowledgments appear on page 96.

ISBN: 0-688-13407-6

Printed in Singapore
First Edition
1 2 3 4 5 6 7 8 9 10

Country Living Staff
Rachel Newman, Editor-in-Chief
Niña Williams, Executive Editor
Julio Vega, Art Director
Mary R. Roby, Managing Editor
John Mack Carter, Director, Magazine Development

Produced by Smallwood and Stewart, Inc., New York City

Edited by Rachel Carley
Designed by Jan Melchior

Contents

Introduction

Once you have experienced that labor of love known as gardening, you'll never understand a life without it. The personal pleasures to be harvested are never-ending, whether you create a salad with vegetables fresh from your garden or cut a bouquet of flowers for a friend who just stopped by.

In Manhattan I don't have the luxury of rich soil and a large backyard to transform into a Garden of Eden. Yet I, like many city dwellers, make do with what I have, enthusiastically tending an expanding collection of houseplants. Gardening, you see, is more than just a hobby, it's a part of life, just as necessary in the concrete metropolis as in the heartland of America.

This journal was created to add to your gardening pleasure—and success—by giving you a place to record your schedules and shopping lists, track your plantings, even jot down your impressions about the passage of the seasons and the beauty of your harvest. We at Country Living *wish you an abundance of flowers in the sunshine and a wealth of memories in your garden journal. Happy planting!*

RACHEL NEWMAN
EDITOR-IN-CHIEF
COUNTRY LIVING

Spring Journal

**But each spring . . .
a gardening instinct, sure as
the sap rising in the trees,
stirs within us.
We look about and decide
to tame another little
bit of ground.**

LEWIS GANNETT

It is astonishing how short a time it takes for very wonderful things to happen.

FRANCES HODGSON BURNETT

Spring Checklist

- ☐ Organize and sharpen tools.
- ☐ Start indoor seed trays and peat pots.
- ☐ Replace dirt in flower pots and window boxes.
- ☐ Clear lawn and beds of fallen branches and other winter debris.
- ☐ Till beds and prepare soil with any needed nutrients, such as fertilizer and mulch.
- ☐ Dethatch and roll lawn.
- ☐ Reseed lawn where needed.

Low-maintenance Annuals

Ageratum (*A. houstonianum*) ➾ Cleome (*C.hasslerana*)

Cockscomb (*Celosia argentea* var. *cristata*) ➾ Coleus (*C. blumei*)

Cosmos (*C. bipinnatus*) ➾ Dianthus (*D. barbatus*)

Flowering Maple (*Abutilon hybridum*) ➾ Gazania (*G. longiscapa*)

Gypsophila (*G. elegans*) ➾ Impatiens (*I. balsamina*)

Larkspur (*Consolida*) ➾ Linaria (*L. maroccana*)

Marigold (*Tagetes*) ➾ Mexican Sunflower (*Tithonia rotundifolia*)

Nasturtium (*Tropaeolum majus*) ➾ Pansy (*Viola* × *wittrockiana*)

Petunia (*Petunia* × *hybrida*) ➾ Phlox (*P. drummondii*)

Portulaca (*P. grandiflora*) ➾ Salvia (*S. horminum*)

Snapdragon (*Antirrhinum majus*) ➾ Statice (*Limonium sinuata*)

Stock (*Matthiola*) ➾ Tahoka Daisy (*Aster tanacetifolius*)

Wax Begonia (*Begonia* × *semperflorens-cultorum*)

Plants for Attracting Butterflies

Aubrieta (*Aubrieta*) ➾ Basket-of-gold (*Aurinia saxatilis*)

Bee Balm (*Monarda didyma*) ➾ Bellflower (*Campanula*)

Blanket Flower (*Gaillardia*) ➾ Butterfly Bush (*Buddleia davidii*)

Cosmos (*C. hybrida*) ➾ Gayfeather (*Liatris spicata*)

Honeysuckle (*Lonicera*) ➾ Johnny-jump-up (*Viola tricolor*)

Lavender (*Lavendula*) ➾ Lilac (*Syringa*)

Lupine (*Lupinus*) ➾ Marigold (*Tagetes*)

Nasturtium (*Tropaeolum majus*) ➾ Passion Flower (*Passiflora*)

Red Valerian (*Centranthus ruber*) ➾ Sage (*Salvia*)

Scabiosa (*S. caucasica*) ➾ Sea Holly (*Eryngium maritimum*)

Shasta Daisy (*Chrysanthemum × superbum*)

Sweet Alyssum (*Lobularia maritima*)

Sweet Pea (*Lathyrus odoratus*) ➾ Zinnia (*Zinnia*)

CALLIOPSIS
FANCY MIXED
DWARF NASTURTIUM
FANCY MIXED
PANSY
FANCY MIXED
10¢
PHLOX
FANCY MIXED

Garden Plotter

Garden Log

To a gardener there
is nothing more
exasperating than
a hose that just
isn't long enough.
CECIL ROBERTS

PLANT

☐ Annual ☐ Perennial ☐ Bulb ☐ Seed

WHERE PURCHASED

WHEN AND WHERE PLANTED

COLOR BLOOM TIME

HEIGHT SPREAD

HOW IT DID

PLANT

☐ Annual ☐ Perennial ☐ Bulb ☐ Seed

WHERE PURCHASED

WHEN AND WHERE PLANTED

COLOR BLOOM TIME

HEIGHT SPREAD

HOW IT DID

PLANT ____________________

☐ Annual ☐ Perennial ☐ Bulb ☐ Seed

WHERE PURCHASED ____________________

WHEN AND WHERE PLANTED ____________________

____

COLOR ____________________ BLOOM TIME ____________________

HEIGHT ____________________ SPREAD ____________________

HOW IT DID ____________________

____

____

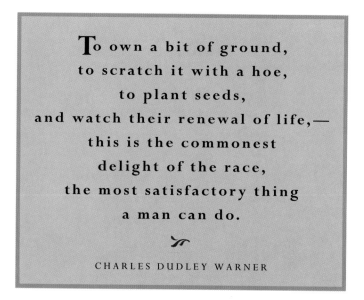

To own a bit of ground,
to scratch it with a hoe,
to plant seeds,
and watch their renewal of life,—
this is the commonest
delight of the race,
the most satisfactory thing
a man can do.

CHARLES DUDLEY WARNER

PLANT________________________________

☐ Annual ☐ Perennial ☐ Bulb ☐ Seed

WHERE PURCHASED__________________________

WHEN AND WHERE PLANTED____________________

COLOR______________ BLOOM TIME______________

HEIGHT______________ SPREAD______________

HOW IT DID____________________________

PLANT________________________________

☐ Annual ☐ Perennial ☐ Bulb ☐ Seed

WHERE PURCHASED__________________________

WHEN AND WHERE PLANTED____________________

COLOR______________ BLOOM TIME______________

HEIGHT______________ SPREAD______________

HOW IT DID____________________________

PLANT ________________________

☐ Annual ☐ Perennial ☐ Bulb ☐ Seed

WHERE PURCHASED ________________________

WHEN AND WHERE PLANTED ________________________

COLOR ____________ BLOOM TIME ____________

HEIGHT ____________ SPREAD ____________

HOW IT DID ________________________

PLANT ________________________

☐ Annual ☐ Perennial ☐ Bulb ☐ Seed

WHERE PURCHASED ________________________

WHEN AND WHERE PLANTED ________________________

COLOR ____________ BLOOM TIME ____________

HEIGHT ____________ SPREAD ____________

HOW IT DID ________________________

First sightings

Plant Date

PLANT ____________________

☐ Annual ☐ Perennial ☐ Bulb ☐ Seed

WHERE PURCHASED ____________________

WHEN AND WHERE PLANTED ____________________

COLOR ____________________ BLOOM TIME ____________________

HEIGHT ____________________ SPREAD ____________________

HOW IT DID ____________________

PLANT ____________________

☐ Annual ☐ Perennial ☐ Bulb ☐ Seed

WHERE PURCHASED ____________________

WHEN AND WHERE PLANTED ____________________

COLOR ____________________ BLOOM TIME ____________________

HEIGHT ____________________ SPREAD ____________________

HOW IT DID ____________________

PLANT____

☐ Annual ☐ Perennial ☐ Bulb ☐ Seed

WHERE PURCHASED________________________________

WHEN AND WHERE PLANTED__________________________

COLOR__________________ BLOOM TIME__________________

HEIGHT__________________ SPREAD__________________

HOW IT DID____________________________________

PLANT____

☐ Annual ☐ Perennial ☐ Bulb ☐ Seed

WHERE PURCHASED________________________________

WHEN AND WHERE PLANTED__________________________

COLOR__________________ BLOOM TIME__________________

HEIGHT__________________ SPREAD__________________

HOW IT DID____________________________________

PLANT ______________________

☐ Annual ☐ Perennial ☐ Bulb ☐ Seed

WHERE PURCHASED ______________________

WHEN AND WHERE PLANTED ______________________

____

COLOR ______________ BLOOM TIME ______________

HEIGHT ______________ SPREAD ______________

HOW IT DID ______________________

____

____

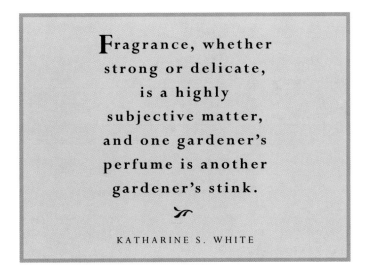

Fragrance, whether strong or delicate, is a highly subjective matter, and one gardener's perfume is another gardener's stink.

KATHARINE S. WHITE

PLANT ______________________________

☐ Annual ☐ Perennial ☐ Bulb ☐ Seed

WHERE PURCHASED ______________________________

WHEN AND WHERE PLANTED ______________________________

____

COLOR ______________ BLOOM TIME ______________

HEIGHT ______________ SPREAD ______________

HOW IT DID ______________________________

____

____

PLANT ______________________________

☐ Annual ☐ Perennial ☐ Bulb ☐ Seed

WHERE PURCHASED ______________________________

WHEN AND WHERE PLANTED ______________________________

____

COLOR ______________ BLOOM TIME ______________

HEIGHT ______________ SPREAD ______________

HOW IT DID ______________________________

____

____

PLANT ______

☐ Annual ☐ Perennial ☐ Bulb ☐ Seed

WHERE PURCHASED ______

WHEN AND WHERE PLANTED ______

______

COLOR ______ BLOOM TIME ______

HEIGHT ______ SPREAD ______

HOW IT DID ______

______

______

PLANT ______

☐ Annual ☐ Perennial ☐ Bulb ☐ Seed

WHERE PURCHASED ______

WHEN AND WHERE PLANTED ______

______

COLOR ______ BLOOM TIME ______

HEIGHT ______ SPREAD ______

HOW IT DID ______

______

______

PRUNING GUIDE

To control vigorous growth:
Prune in summer or fall.

To encourage a bud to grow:
Make a pruning cut just above the bud or at the base of a branch. The face of the cut should slope away from the bud.

To rejuvenate an overgrown flowering shrub:
Remove about one third of the oldest wood; cut close to the ground.

To remove a branch:
Prune with a pruning saw or with long-handled lopping shears. Cut just above the branch collar (the swelling at the base of the branch). Do not cut flush with the trunk.

To produce a vigorous burst of growth during the next season:
Prune during the dormant season.

To prune a hedge:
Trim after major spring growth,
then as often as needed to keep the hedge neat.

To prune spring-flowering shrubs:
Make cuts immediately after they bloom.

To prune summer-flowering shrubs:
Make cuts in the late winter or early spring.

To prune fall-flowering shrubs:
Make cuts when dormant, usually in late winter.

CONTAINER PLANT SHOPPING LIST

PLANT ____________________

CONTAINER USED ____________________

NUMBER OF FLATS/POTS NEEDED ____________________

PLANT ____________________

CONTAINER USED ____________________

NUMBER OF FLATS/POTS NEEDED ____________________

PLANT ____________________

CONTAINER USED ____________________

NUMBER OF FLATS/POTS NEEDED ____________________

PLANT ____________________

CONTAINER USED ____________________

NUMBER OF FLATS/POTS NEEDED ____________________

PLANT ____________________

CONTAINER USED ____________________

NUMBER OF FLATS/POTS NEEDED ____________________

PLANT ______

CONTAINER USED ______

NUMBER OF FLATS/POTS NEEDED ______

PLANT ______

CONTAINER USED ______

NUMBER OF FLATS/POTS NEEDED ______

PLANT ______

CONTAINER USED ______

NUMBER OF FLATS/POTS NEEDED ______

PLANT ______

CONTAINER USED ______

NUMBER OF FLATS/POTS NEEDED ______

PLANT ______

CONTAINER USED ______

NUMBER OF FLATS/POTS NEEDED ______

PLANT ______

CONTAINER USED ______

NUMBER OF FLATS/POTS NEEDED ______

GOOD PLANTS FOR CONTAINERS

Blue Lace Flower (*Trachymene coerulea*)

Bush Violet (*Browallia*) ➾ Catmint (*Nepeta mussinii*)

Chive (*Allium schoenoprasum*) ➾ Dahlia (*Dahlia*)

Gladiolus (*Gladiolus*) ➾ Grape Hyacinth (*Muscari*)

Impatiens (*I. wallerana*) ➾ Lamb's Ear (*Stachys byzantina*)

Lavender (*Lavendula*) ➾ Lily (*Lilium*)

Mint (*Mentha*) ➾ Narcissus (*Narcissus*)

Nemesia (*Nemesia*) ➾ Ornamental Kale (*Brassica oleracea*)

Pansy (*Viola* × *wittrockiana*) ➾ Petunia (*Petunia* × *hybrida*)

Phlox (*P. drummondi*) ➾ Pot Marigold (*Calendula officinalis*)

Rosemary (*Rosmarinus officinalis*)

Snapdragon (*Antirrhinum majus*) ➾ Strawberry (*Fragaria*)

Sweet Alyssum (*Lobularia maritima*) ➾ Tulip (*Tulipa*)

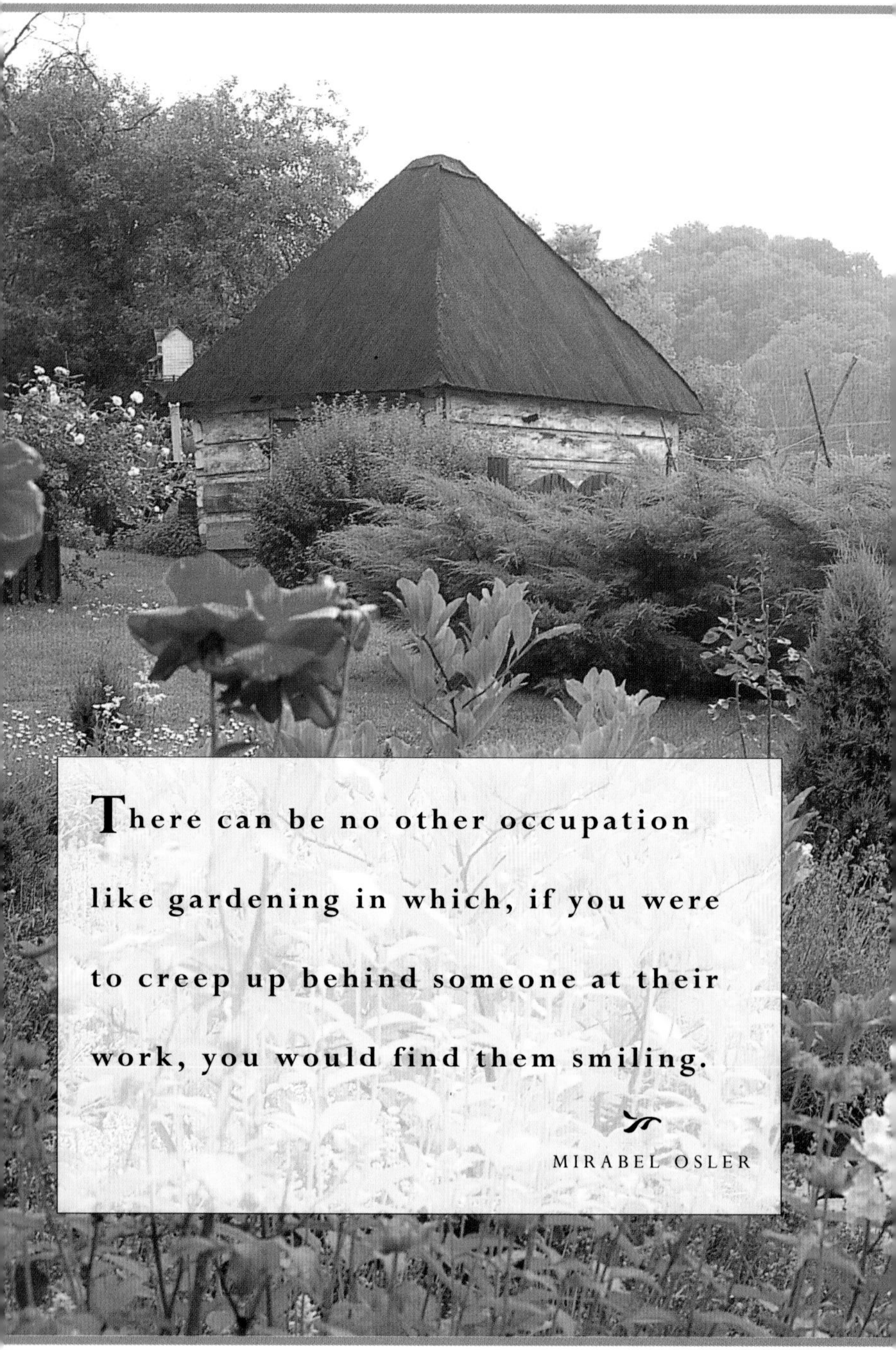

There can be no other occupation like gardening in which, if you were to creep up behind someone at their work, you would find them smiling.

MIRABEL OSLER

Summer Journal

Give me the splendid silent sun with all his beams full-dazzling!

WALT WHITMAN

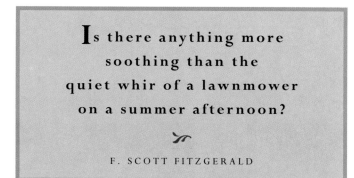

Is there anything more soothing than the quiet whir of a lawnmower on a summer afternoon?

F. SCOTT FITZGERALD

I cried at first . . .
. . . and then, it was
such a beautiful day,
that I forgot
to be unhappy.

FRANCES NOYES HART

NOTES ON MY VEGETABLE GARDEN

Plant ______

Comments ______

______

Plant ______

Comments ______

______

Plant ______

Comments ______

______

Plant ______

Comments ______

______

Plant ______

Comments ______

______

Plant

Comments

Plant

Comments

Plant

Comments

Plant

Comments

Plant

Comments

Plant

Comments

A man full of words and not of deeds is like a garden full of weeds.

ANONYMOUS

Sweet childish days, that were as long

As twenty days are now.

WILLIAM WORDSWORTH

Gifts from My Garden

Gift ______________________________

To whom ______________________________

Date/Occasion ______________________________

Gift ______________________________

To whom ______________________________

Date/Occasion ______________________________

Gift ______________________________

To whom ______________________________

Date/Occasion ______________________________

Gift ______________________________

To whom ______________________________

Date/Occasion ______________________________

Gift ______________________________

To whom ______________________________

Date/Occasion ______________________________

Gift ______________________________

To whom ______________________________

Date/Occasion ______________________________

Gift ____________________

To whom ____________________

Date/Occasion ____________________

Gift ____________________

To whom ____________________

Date/Occasion ____________________

Gift ____________________

To whom ____________________

Date/Occasion ____________________

Gift ____________________

To whom ____________________

Date/Occasion ____________________

Gift ____________________

To whom ____________________

Date/Occasion ____________________

Gift ____________________

To whom ____________________

Date/Occasion ____________________

Gift ______________________________

To whom ______________________________

Date/Occasion ______________________________

Gift ______________________________

To whom ______________________________

Date/Occasion ______________________________

Gift ______________________________

To whom ______________________________

Date/Occasion ______________________________

Gift ______________________________

To whom ______________________________

Date/Occasion ______________________________

Gift ______________________________

To whom ______________________________

Date/Occasion ______________________________

Gift ______________________________

To whom ______________________________

Date/Occasion ______________________________

Plants for Drying

Artemisia (*Artemisia*) ➾ Baby's Breath (*Gypsophila paniculata*)

Bee Balm (*Monarda didyma*) ➾ Bishop's Flower (*Ammimajus*)

Blanket Flower (*Gaillardia*) ➾ Chive (*Allium Schoenoprasum*)

Cockscomb (*Celosia argentea* var. *cristata*) ➾ Delphinium

(*Delphinium* × *cultorum*) ➾ Everlasting (*Helipterum roseum*)

Fountain Grass (*Pennisetum alopecuroides* 'Burgundy Giant')

Gayfeather (*Liatris*) ➾ Globe Thistle (*Echinops ritro*)

Honesty (*Lynaria annua*) ➾ Heather (*Calluna*)

Lavender (*Lavandula angustifolia*) ➾ Loosestrife (*Lythrum*)

Love-lies-bleeding (*Amaranthus caudatus*) ➾ Peony (*Paeonia*)

Periwinkle (*Vinca*) ➾ Russian Sage (*Perovskia atriplicifolia*)

Scabiosa (*S. stellata*) ➾ Spearmint (*Mentha spicata*)

Strawflower (*Helichrysum bracteatum*) ➾ Thyme (*Thymus*)

Thrift (*Armeria*) ➾ Yarrow (*Achillea*)

Autumn Journal

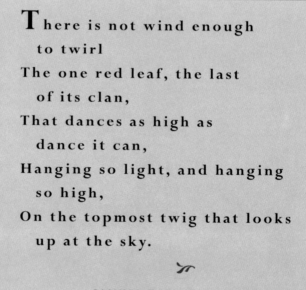

There is not wind enough
  to twirl
The one red leaf, the last
  of its clan,
That dances as high as
  dance it can,
Hanging so light, and hanging
  so high,
On the topmost twig that looks
  up at the sky.

SAMUEL TAYLOR COLERIDGE

SHRUBS FOR AUTUMN COLOR

American Cranberrybush (*Biburnum trilobum*), red berries and foliage

Arrowwood Viburnum (*V. dentatum*), red foliage, blue-black berries

Cranberry Cotoneaster (*C. apiculatus*), scarlet berries

Doublefile Viburnum (*V. plicatum* var. *tomentosum*), red-purple foliage

Ghent Hybrid Azalea (*Rhododendron × gandavense 'Corneille'*), red-purple foliage

Golden Currant (*Ribes aureum*), yellow-orange foliage

Large Fothergilla (*F. major*), red foliage

Nannyberry (*Viburnum lentago*), blue-black berries

Purple Beautyberry (*Callicarpa dichotoma*), dark red berries

Sapphire Berry (*Symplocos paniculata*), blue berries

Staghorn Sumac (*Rhus typhina*), red foliage

Autumn Checklist

- ☐ Bring indoors any plants you plan to winter over.
- ☐ Dig and till new perennial beds to allow them to settle over the winter.
- ☐ Dig up summer-blooming bulbs not hardy for your region and store in bags of peat in a cool, dry place where they won't freeze.
- ☐ In a cold climate with a dry fall, thoroughly water shrubs twice a week before winter sets in.
- ☐ Wrap unprotected broadleaf evergreens in burlap or other loose covering.
- ☐ Protect new perennials with a loose covering of hay.
- ☐ Clean and store tools.
- ☐ Order seed catalogs.

Catalogs catalogs . . .

Company

Phone number

Notes

Company

Phone number

Notes

Company

Phone number

Notes

Company

Phone number

Notes

Company

Phone number

Notes

Company

Phone number

Notes

A worm is as good a traveler as a grasshopper or a cricket, and a much wiser settler.

HENRY DAVID THOREAU

Company

Phone number

Notes

Company

Phone number

Notes

Winter Journal

I value my garden more
for being full of blackbirds
than of cherries,
and very frankly give them
fruit for their songs.

JOSEPH ADDISON

Thoughts for Next Year

January..................Snow Month

February................Rain Month

March...................Wind Month

April.....................Bud Month

May..................Flower Month

June.....................Heat Month

July.......................Hay Month

August...............Harvest Month

September...............Fruit Month

October................Grape Month

November................Fog Month

December...............Winter Month

From an old Quaker calendar